AF584456

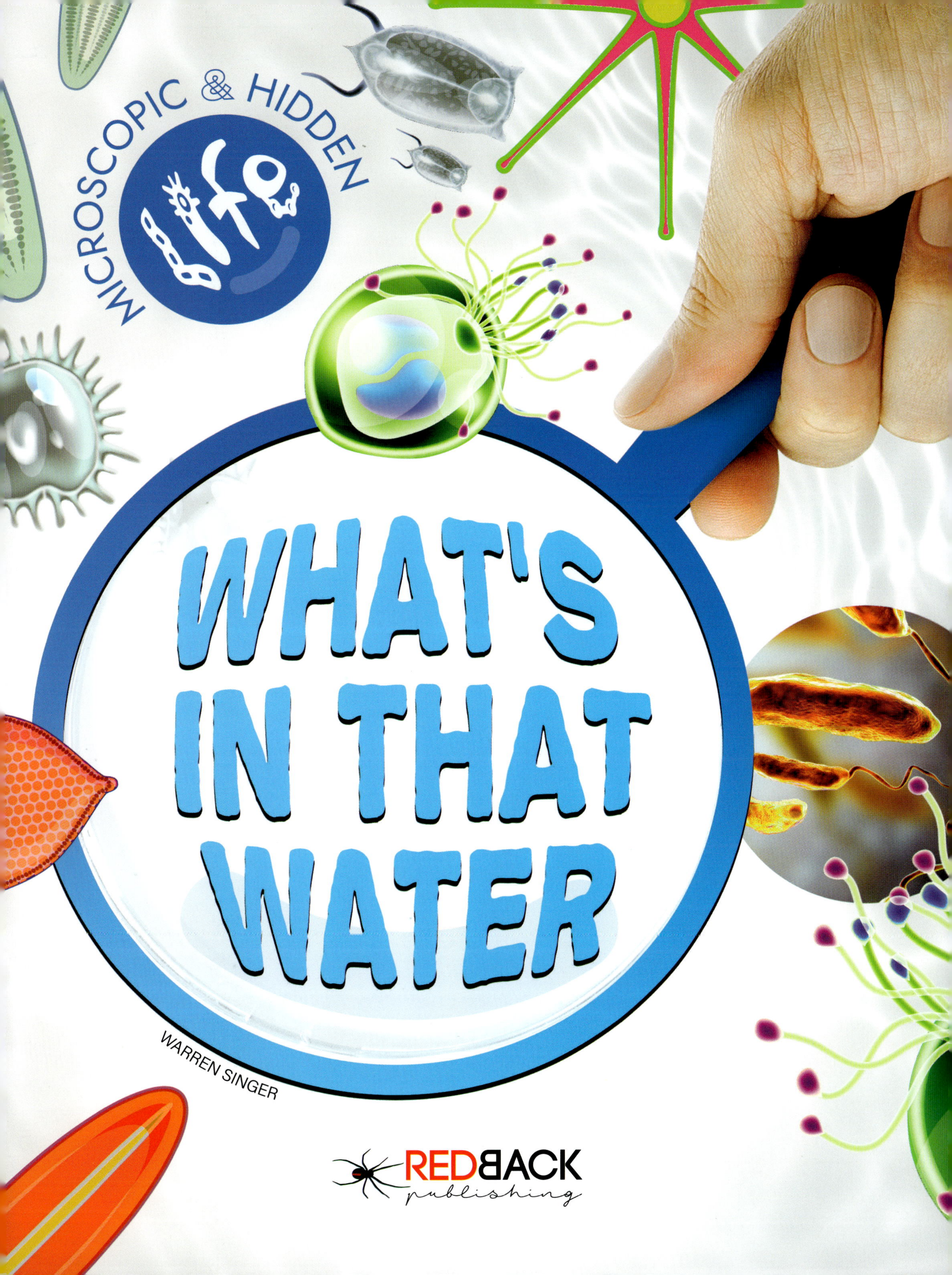
MICROSCOPIC & HIDDEN
life
WHAT'S IN THAT WATER
WARREN SINGER
REDBACK
publishing

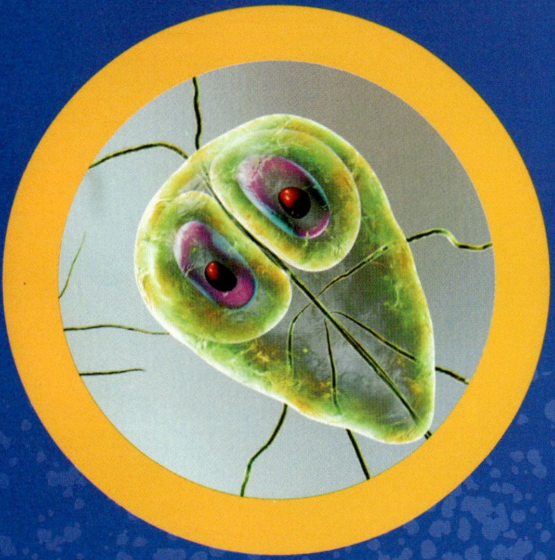

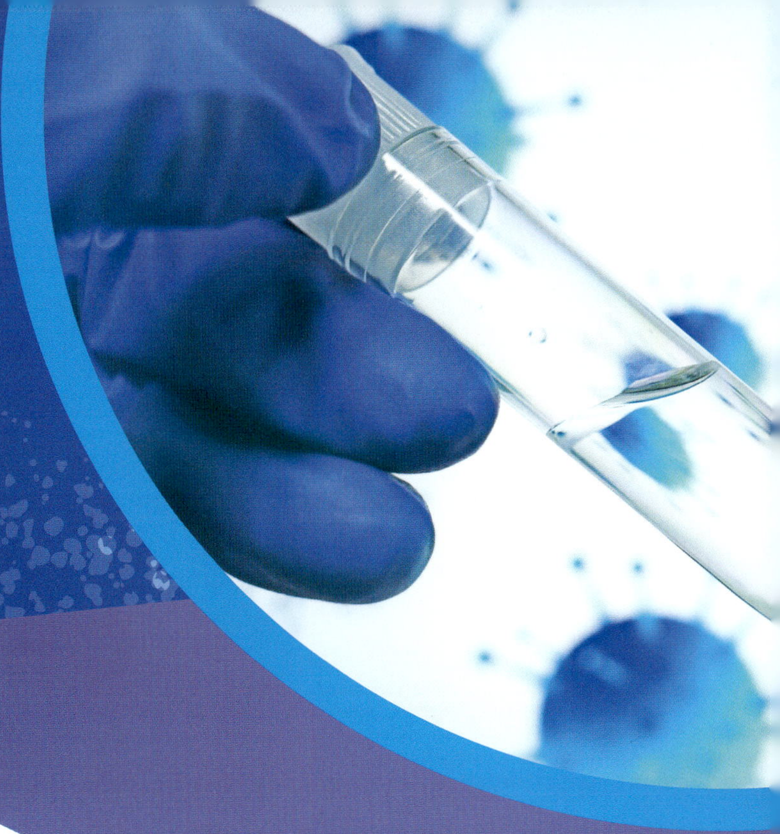

First Published 2026 by
Redback Publishing
Suite 6, 13a Narabang Way,
Belrose NSW 2085
Australia

www.redbackpublishing.com
orders@redbackpublishing.com

ISBN 978-1-761401-29-9

Author: Warren Singer
Editors: Lucinda Dodds and Emma Dobinson
Designer: Redback Publishing

MIX
Paper from responsible sources
FSC™ C001507
www.fsc.org

Original illustrations © Redback Publishing 2026
Originated by Redback Publishing

Acknowledgements
Abbreviations: l—left, r—right, b—bottom, t—top, c—centre, m—middle
We would like to thank the following for permission to reproduce photographs: (Images © shutterstock, Alamy) p11m - © Hans Hillewaert / CC BY-SA 4.0, p13br - NASA Johnson Space Center, Public domain, via Wikimedia Commons, p15tl - National Marine Sanctuaries, Public domain, via Wikimedia Commons, p15mr - © Hans Hillewaert / CC BY-SA 4.0, p21tr - CSIRO, CC BY 3.0 <https://creativecommons.org/licenses/by/3.0>, via Wikimedia Commons, p21mr - Wipeter, CC BY-SA 3.0 <http://creativecommons.org/licenses/by-sa/3.0/>, via Wikimedia Commons, p23mr - Silke Baron, CC BY 2.0 <https://creativecommons.org/licenses/by/2.0>, via Wikimedia Commons, p25bl - Chiswick Chap - Own work, CC BY-SA 3.0, https://commons.wikimedia.org/w/index.php?curid=26202020, p29ml - Annaleida, CC BY-SA 4.0 <https://creativecommons.org/licenses/by-sa/4.0>, via Wikimedia Commons

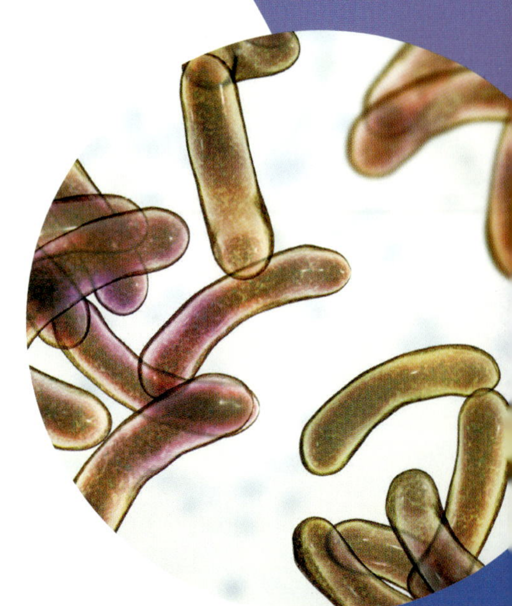

A catalogue record for this book is available from the National Library of Australia

CONTENTS

WATER IS ALIVE!

Life on Earth needs water to survive. Humans drink it, swim in it, wash in it and use it to water gardens and fill swimming pools. But what is hidden in that water?

Water is more than a drink to billions of living things that we cannot see. It is their home and probably the only place in the Universe where they can survive.

The microscopic world of water includes bacteria, fungi, viruses, protozoans, as well as algae, fish and coral eggs, as well as tiny creatures with legs, eyes and whole life cycles that we know very little about.

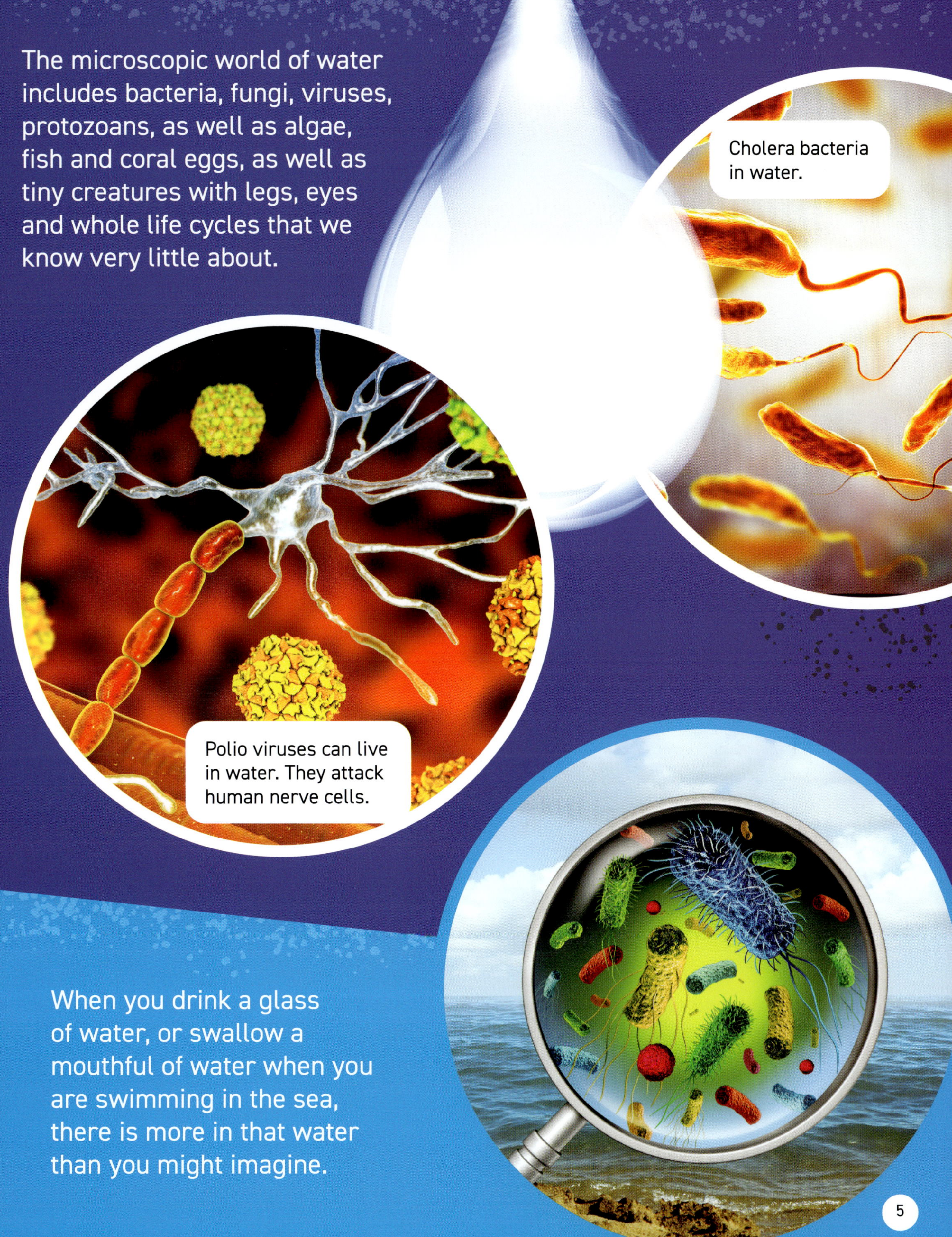

Cholera bacteria in water.

Polio viruses can live in water. They attack human nerve cells.

When you drink a glass of water, or swallow a mouthful of water when you are swimming in the sea, there is more in that water than you might imagine.

TAP WATER

The safety of tap water for drinking depends on where the water comes from.

RAINWATER

Rainwater stored in tanks is likely to have many microorganisms in it. These are washed off the roof into the tank, they may be growing in the tank, or they may have been collected from the air as the rain fell.

WATER SUPPLY AUTHORITIES

These organisations test drinking water. They have methods for killing most of the microorganisms that may be in the water that flows through pipes to taps in homes.

RIVERS AND LAKES

Water taken directly out of rivers and lakes is likely to be full of microorganisms. Some of these will be harmless to people, while others can be deadly.

We divide microbes in water into good and bad, depending on how they affect us as humans.

DANGEROUS MICROORGANISMS IN WATER	
E. coli	Danger to health. Present when water is contaminated by faeces.
Protozoans	*Cryptosporidium* and *Giardia* cause intestinal illnesses.
Adenoviruses	Cause colds and flu.
Hepatitis virus	Causes serious liver infections.
Norovirus	Causes 'stomach flu'.

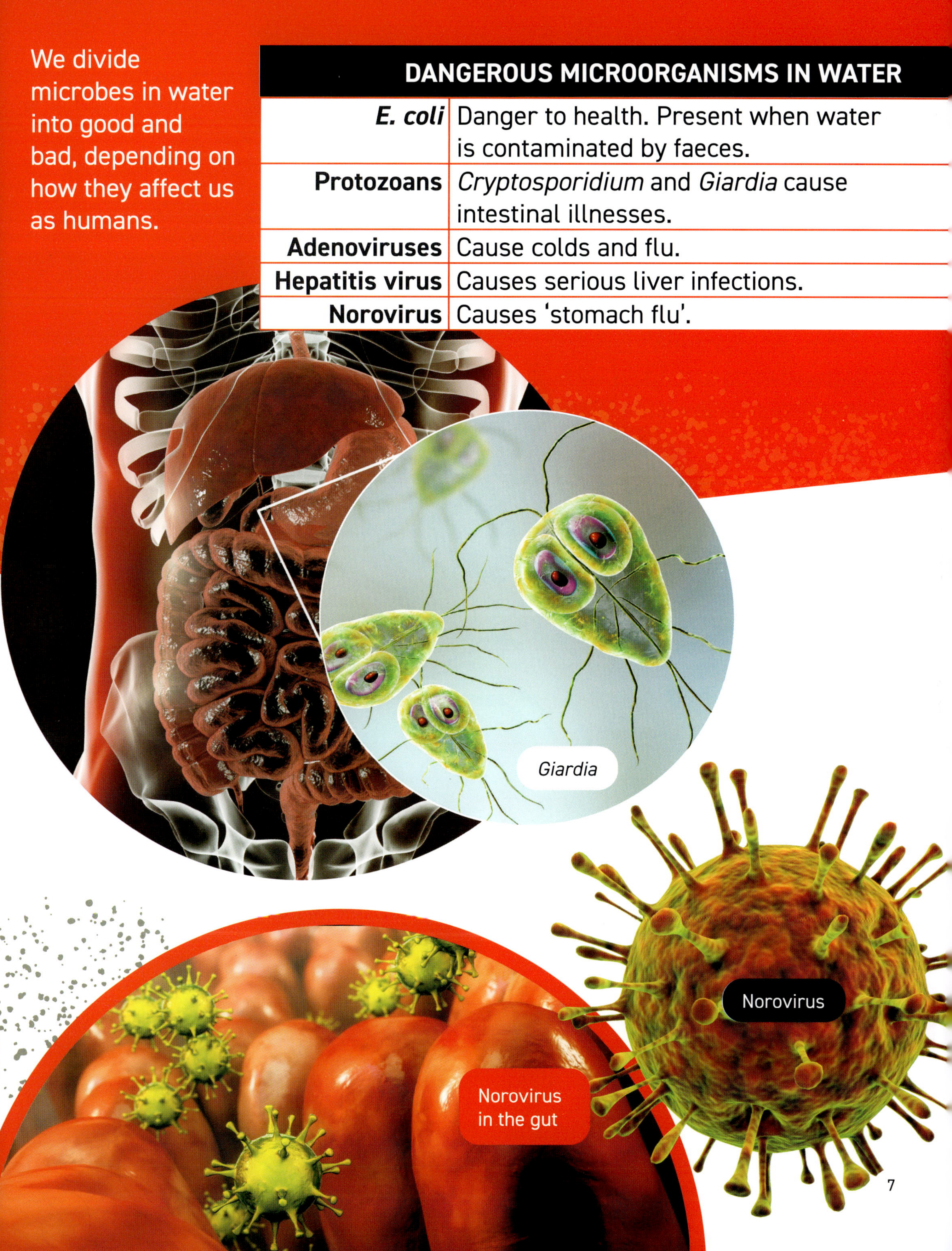

Giardia

Norovirus

Norovirus in the gut

SAFE WATER

How do we make water safe to drink?

Water without any living things in it is called sterile. Water can be sterilised with chemicals, or by using UV light or gamma radiation.

Water treatment plant

Boiling water does not kill everything in it, but it does get rid of most of the bugs that can make us sick. Filtering water does not remove the tiniest viruses.

Some bacteria, viruses and protozoans can survive being in hot water, or the effect of adding chlorine to water. These include the protozoan *Cryptosporidium*, (which causes serious stomach upsets), and the anthrax bacteria, (which cause illness in animals and humans).

POO IN WATER

All living things, including fish, plankton and humans, produce waste. A lot of this waste, or poo, ends up in water, where it breaks down into chemicals. When we go swimming in natural water, such as the ocean or lakes, we cannot avoid swallowing some of this waste.

COPEPODS

These tiny aquatic creatures are related to prawns, but some only grow to one or two millimetres long. Their larvae are even smaller!

Copepods live in rivers and lakes, as well as in the ocean. You probably had a lot of them in your mouth the last time you were swimming in a river or the sea.

Copepods form one of the Earth's major food sources for other aquatic life. A number of copepods are parasitic on fish, but others eat single-celled plants that are part of plankton in water.

Copepod attached to the gills of a fish.

Copepod with eggs.

To stop them ending up in a cup of tea, copepods have to be filtered out of public water supplies that come from rivers and lakes.

WATER BEARS

Water bears are minuscule creatures called tardigrades, ancient little animals that live and thrive in nearly every habitat in the world.

With common names like moss piglet or water bear, you would expect tardigrades to be cute and cuddly. If they were as big as us, they would be the scariest monsters you could imagine. Fortunately, they are tiny, with the smallest ones being well under a millimetre long.

Tardigrades are stout, with a circular mouth and no face. Their four pairs of stubby legs, each with claws, move them around slowly in search of food. There are well over a thousand different types of tardigrade.

Studying water bears in space.

TINY EXTREMOPHILES

Tardigrades flown into space managed to survive after being taken outside the spaceship! Tardigrades in the deep ocean flourish where other life would be squashed by the pressure, or killed by the heat coming from volcanic vents in the ocean floor.

PLANKTON

Plankton are the plants, animals, bacteria and viruses that drift with currents and tides in water.

Although most of the living things that make up plankton are microscopic, there are a few very large creatures, such as jellyfish, that drift wherever a current takes them.

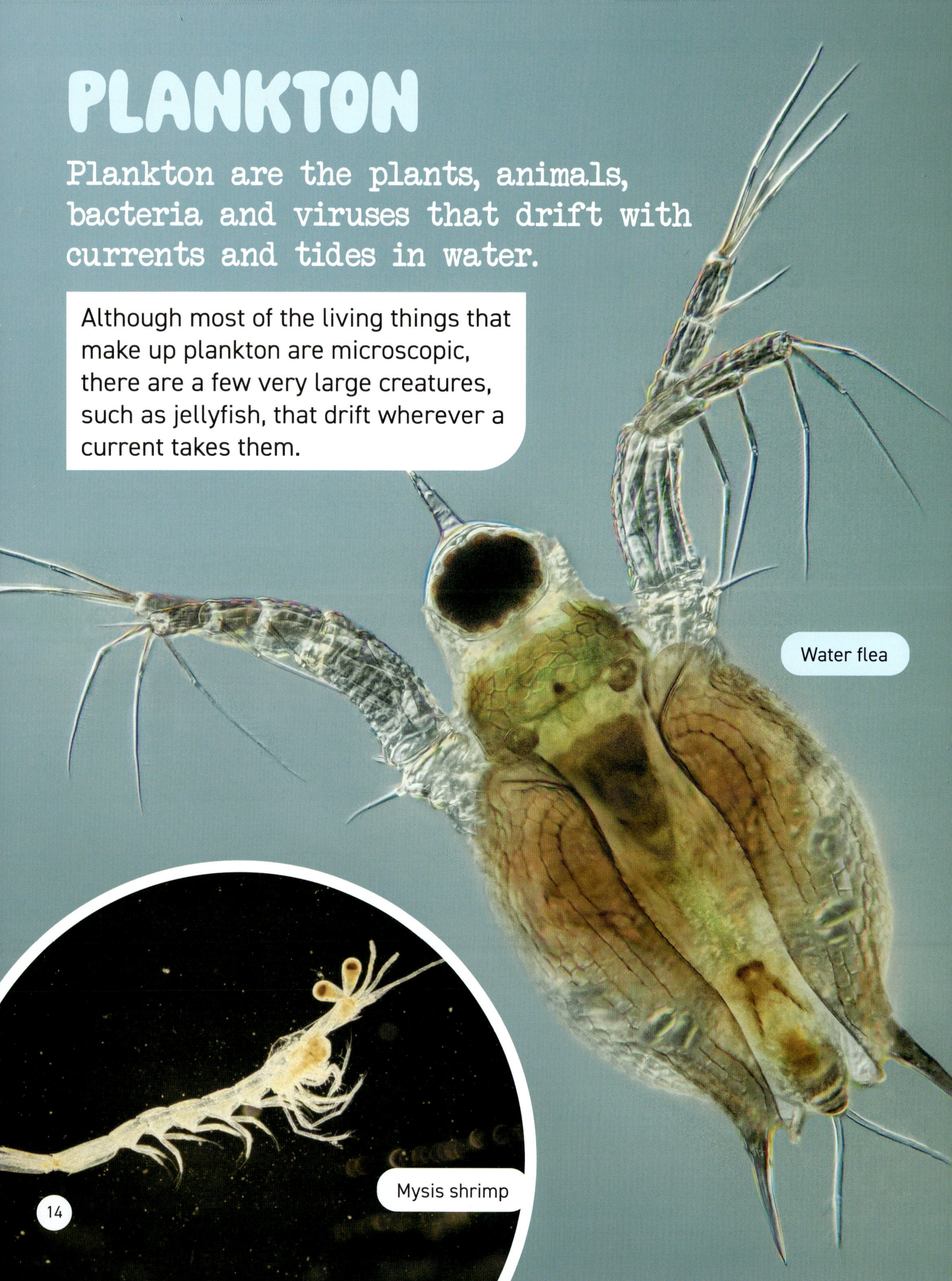

Water flea

Mysis shrimp

Coral eggs

Squid larva

Zooplankton

ZOOPLANKTON

These animals include water snails, shrimp, krill, diatoms and the larval stages of bigger animals such as crabs, octopuses and starfish. Fish eggs and coral eggs are also included amongst plankton.

Crustacean

Blue whale

Zooplankton are food for much of the life in the seas. For example, tiny krill are the main food eaten by gigantic blue whales.

PHYTOPLANKTON

Phytoplankton are microscopic plants that float at the upper layer of the water, where they use energy from sunlight. They are vital for producing oxygen and releasing it into the air. Oxygen is the gas that nearly all life on Earth needs to survive.

Green algae

Phytoplankton includes green algae, diatoms, dinoflagellates and cyanobacteria.

VIRUSES

There are more individual virus particles than any other living thing in aquatic habitats around the world.

Viruses are everywhere, including in water. Some of them are called bacteriophages, and they attack bacteria amongst the plankton. There can be millions of viruses in just one drop of water.

Because the viruses floating with other plankton are so mind-bendingly small, it is very difficult for scientists to count or study them in water.

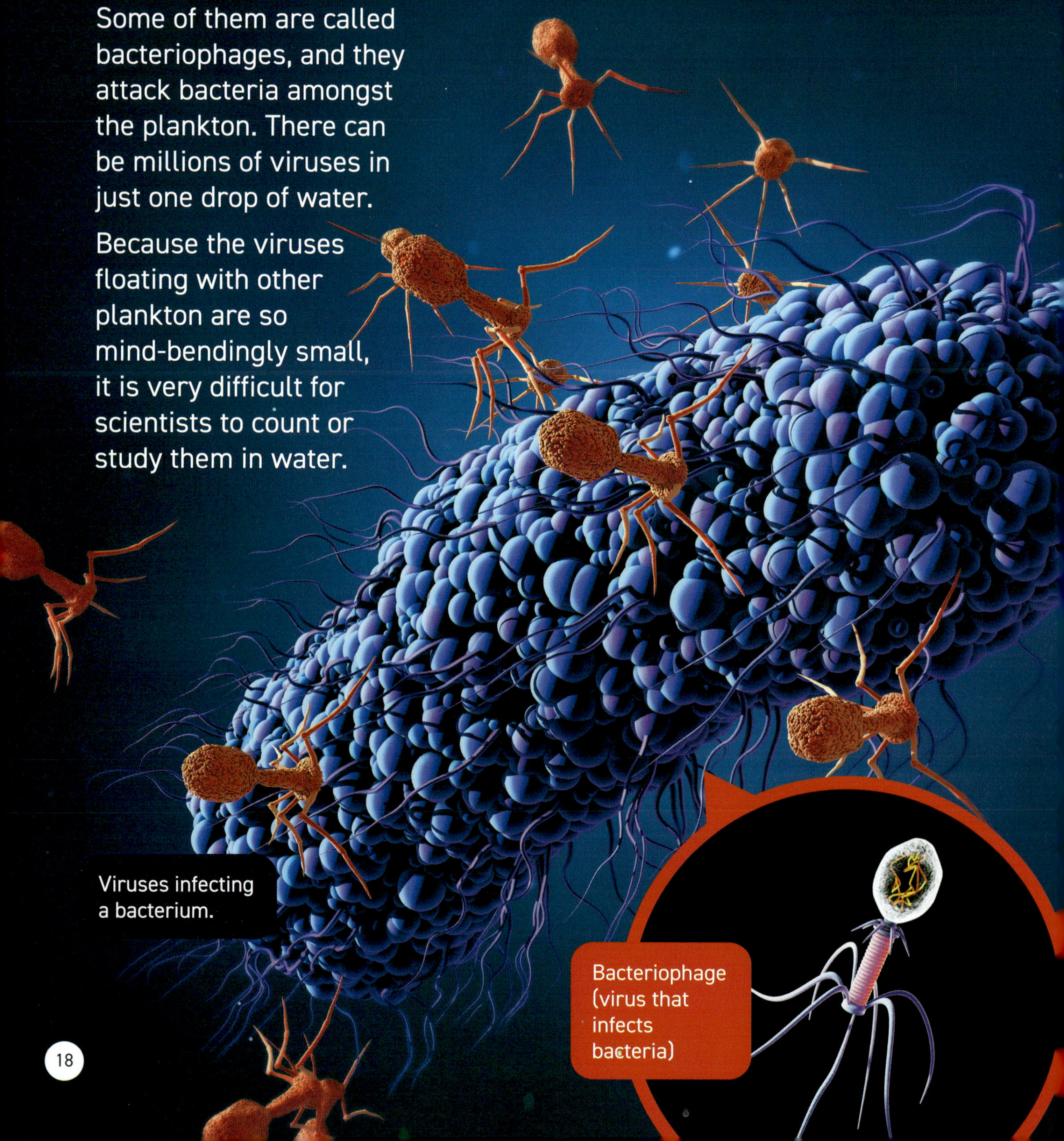

Viruses infecting a bacterium.

Bacteriophage (virus that infects bacteria)

VIRAL DISEASES

There are many diseases of humans and animals that are caused by swallowing viruses in drinking water. These viruses include the ones that cause hepatitis, stomach upsets and polio.

Vaccination can defend us against some viral illnesses.

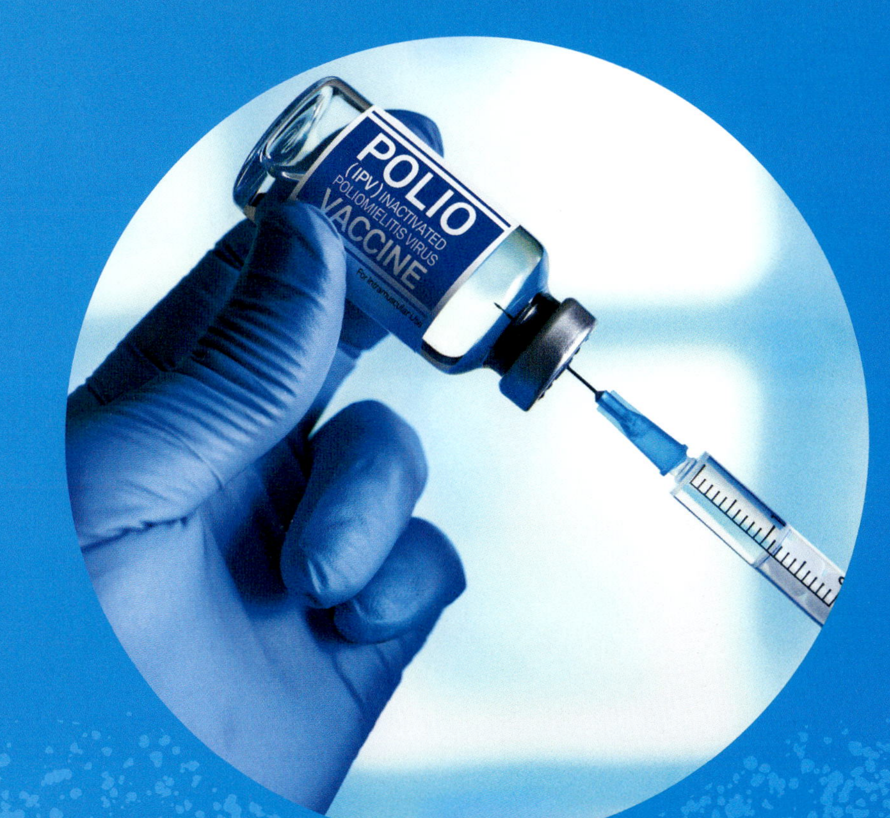

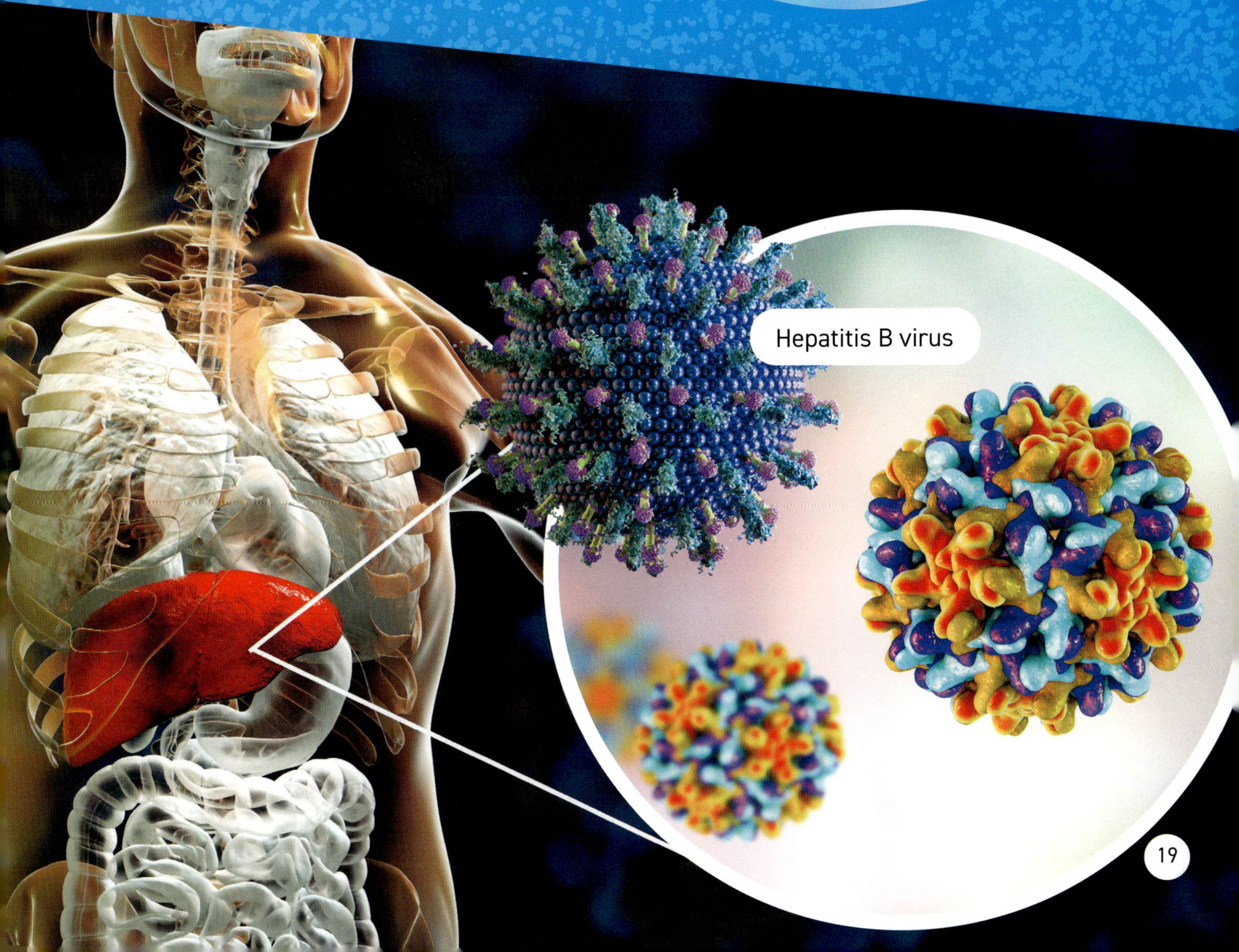

Hepatitis B virus

DIATOMS

Diatoms are important to life on Earth, as they produce 20-50% of the air we breathe.

Diatoms are tiny single-celled algae with clear, hard silica shells formed from the water's chemicals. The largest are about as wide as a human hair. They're everywhere in the ocean, and you've probably swallowed thousands while swimming!

The shells of dead diatoms make deposits hundreds of metres thick on some parts of the ocean floor. They also live in rivers and damp soil.

FISH LARVAE

Fish lay soft, jelly-filled eggs that can be half a millimetre to a few centimetres wide.

Newly-hatched fish larva

Fish eggs float around as part of the plankton, or they may settle and become attached to a rock or plant until they hatch. The baby fish are called larvae, but they are not like the larvae of insects. Fish larvae do not look like their parents at all.

Salmon fish larvae

Fish eggs

Anemone fish eggs

Tilapia fish larvae

Some fish larvae still have a ball of yellow egg yolk in their bellies. They live on this until they can start finding food for themselves.

Sturgeon fish eggs are called caviar, and some people find them delicious.

CRAB AND STARFISH LARVAE

Crabs in the sea lay eggs that hatch into tiny larvae that look nothing like an adult crab.

Crab with eggs

Crab larvae are so tiny that they form part of the floating plankton in the oceans. The smallest ones are less than a millimetre long and impossible to see without a microscope.

Crab larva

Crab larvae are so varied and strange, that for many years scientists thought they were not related to adult crabs and were a completely different form of life.

Starfish larvae look like they could be alien creatures from outer space.

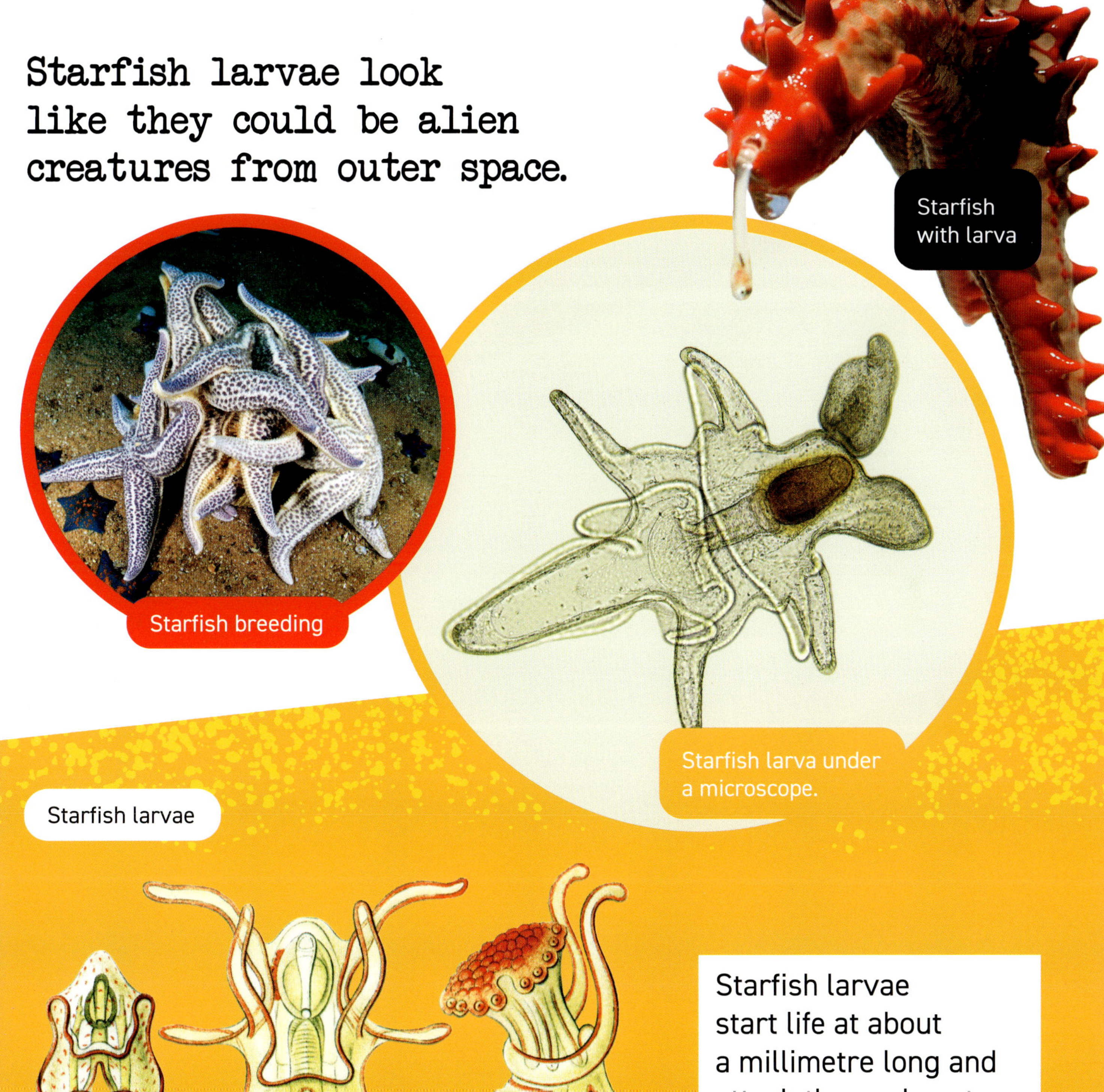

Starfish with larva

Starfish breeding

Starfish larva under a microscope.

Starfish larvae

Starfish larvae start life at about a millimetre long and attach themselves to the sea floor. They stay there until they are big enough to swim freely and have a better chance of escaping from predators.

ROTIFERS

Rotifers are part of the plankton that floats in aquatic environments, although some of them live attached to surfaces under the water, catching food as it flows past them.

Although rotifers are tiny, with most of them being less than a millimetre long, they can be ferocious feeders. They have hard mouthparts surrounded by a ring of moving hairs, called cilia, that draw food into the mouth. If a rotifer were as big as a crocodile, it would be terrifying.

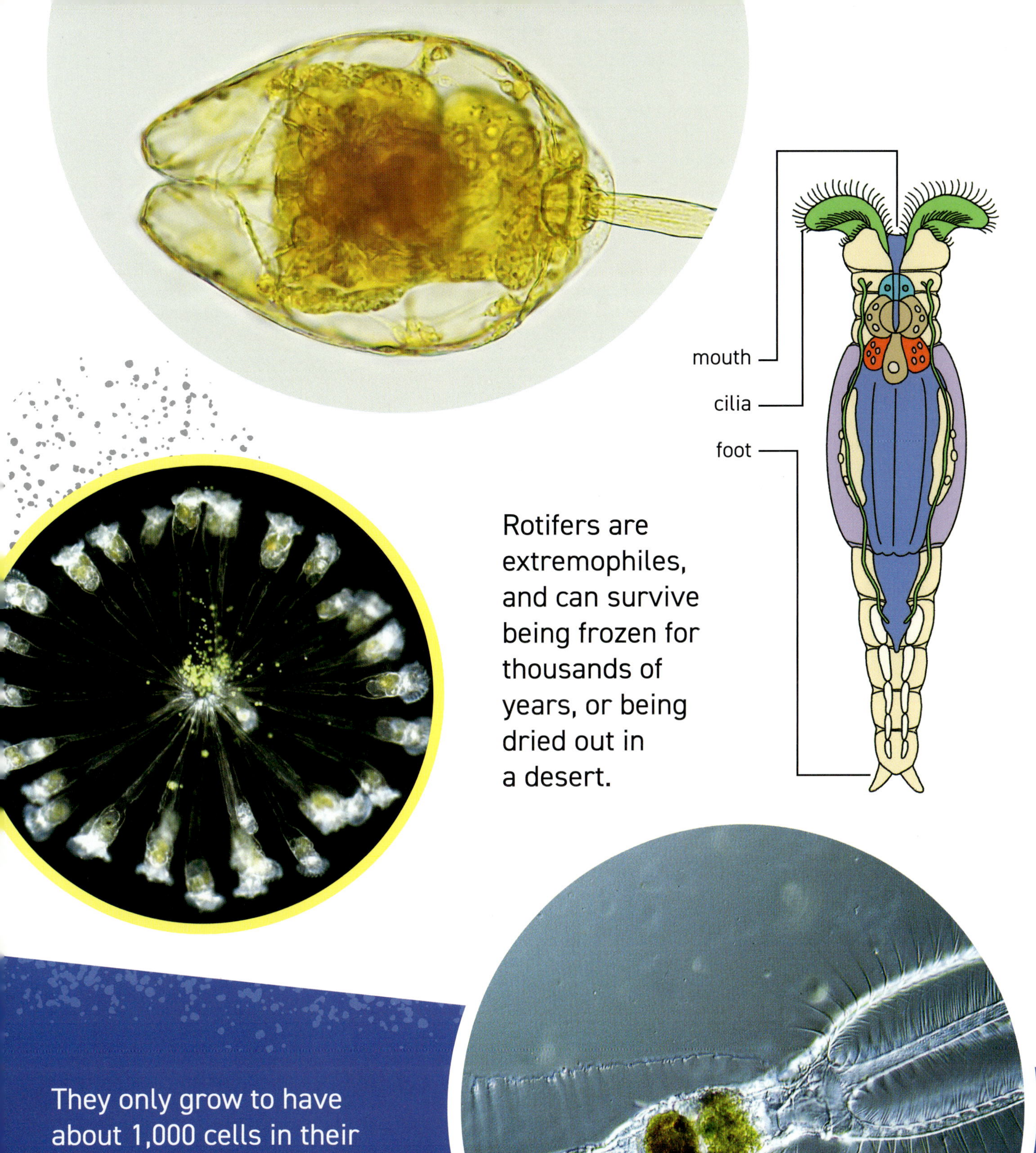

Rotifers are extremophiles, and can survive being frozen for thousands of years, or being dried out in a desert.

They only grow to have about 1,000 cells in their body. Despite this, they have a wide variety of body types and lifestyles, which is remarkable for a living thing that is so small.

SEA SNOT

Also called sea saliva or marine mucilage, sea snot is a foamy, brown scum that appears on the surface of the sea and is often washed onto beaches.

Sea snot is caused by a mixture of plankton and chemicals in the water, such as fertilisers that have been washed into the ocean from rivers. The warming of oceans through climate change makes sea snot worse.

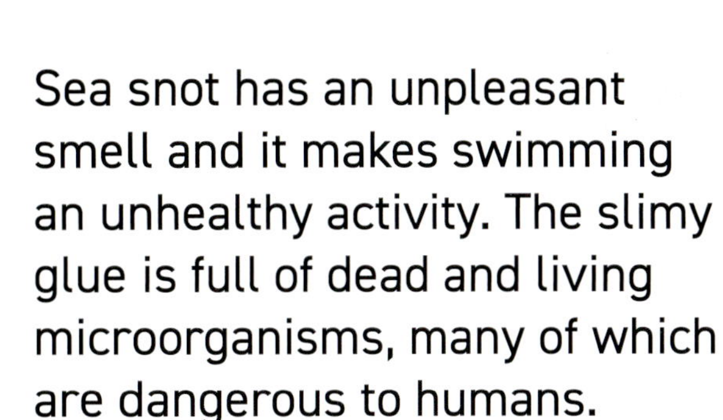

Sea snot has an unpleasant smell and it makes swimming an unhealthy activity. The slimy glue is full of dead and living microorganisms, many of which are dangerous to humans.

This sort of brown foam also occurs in rivers, lakes and dams, so take care whenever you are swimming in water, whether in the sea or in lakes and rivers. Stay out of the water if there is any brown scum on the surface.

IMMUNITY Q & A

QUESTION Since there are so many microscopic things living in water, why aren't we all constantly sick from swallowing them?

White blood cell attacking invaders in an animal body.

ANSWER Humans and other animals have very clever immune systems that can protect us from infections. Some of the tiny creatures that live in water are not interested in using our bodies as a place to live and breed, so they cause us no harm at all.

We have all evolved together over millions of years, and we tend to live in harmony with the microscopic life surrounding us. Sometimes, a microorganism changes into a form that we cannot overcome, and then we get sick. The COVID-19 virus pandemic is a recent example of this happening.

MICROPLASTICS

Water on Earth is teeming with mysterious and amazing living things. There is something else in oceans, rivers and lakes that is not alive, but that is everywhere and just as microscopic as plankton… microplastics!

Microplastics on a beach.

Plastic polluting the ocean stays there, breaking down into tiny pieces. These particles are small enough to get into the gills and flesh of all sorts of aquatic animals, including the ones we like to eat.

Microplastics are already in the drinking water in some parts of the world, where their effect on humans is not yet known for certain.

GLOSSARY

algae simple and often single-celled plants
bacteriophage virus that eats bacteria
cilia hair-like structures that grow on a living thing and move back and forth
contaminated containing infectious or poisonous things
extremophile living thing that can survive in very harsh conditions
immune system body's method of resisting infections
microbe microscopic life form
microorganism life form that cannot be seen with the naked eye
microscopic seen under a microscope
minuscule tiny
protozoan single-celled animal life form
scum dirty layer on top of water
UV light light that we cannot see but that is dangerous to life

INDEX